RIHANNA

POP STAR

KATIE LAJINESS

Big Buddy Books

An Imprint of Abdo Publishing
abdopublishing.com

BIG
BUDDY  BIOGRAPHIES

abdopublishing.com

Printed in the United States of America, North Mankato, Minnesota.
052017
092017

 THIS BOOK CONTAINS
RECYCLED MATERIALS

Cover Photo: Brad Barket/Invision/AP.
Interior Photos: ASSOCIATED PRESS (pp. 6, 9, 25, 29); dpa picture alliance archive/Alamy Stock
    Photo (p. 15); Eric Charbonneau/Invision/AP (p. 27); Everett Collection/Shutterstock.com (p. 9);
    Noel Vasquez/Contributor/Getty (p. 21); REUTERS/Alamy Stock Photo (pp. 11, 13, 17, 23); Sipa
    USA via AP (p. 19); The Photo Access/Alamy Stock Photo (p. 5); WENN Ltd/Alamy Stock Photo
    (p. 25); ZUMA Press, Inc./Alamy Stock Photo (p. 19).

Coordinating Series Editor: Tamara L. Britton
Graphic Design: Jenny Christensen

Publisher's Cataloging-in-Publication Data

Names: Lajiness, Katie, author.
Title: Rihanna / by Katie Lajiness.
Description: Minneapolis, MN : Abdo Publishing, 2018. | Series: Big buddy
    pop biographies | Includes bibliographical references and index.
Identifiers: LCCN 2016962364 | ISBN 9781532110627 (lib. bdg.) |
    ISBN 9781680788471 (ebook)
Subjects: LCSH: Rihanna--Juvenile literature. | Singers--Barbados--
    Biography--Juvenile literature.
Classification: DDC 782.42164092 [B]--dc23
LC record available at http://lccn.loc.gov/2016962364

CONTENTS

POP STAR

Rihanna is a **pop** and **rhythm and blues** singer. She is known for her unique singing voice and fashion sense.

With hit albums and songs, Rihanna's music is popular around the world. She has won many **awards** for her music!

SNAPSHOT

NAME:
Robyn Rihanna Fenty

BIRTHDAY:
February 20, 1988

BIRTHPLACE:
Saint Michael Parish,
Barbados

POPULAR ALBUMS:
Anti, Loud, Talk That Talk

FAMILY TIES

Rihanna's full name is Robyn Rihanna Fenty. She was born in Saint Michael Parish, Barbados, on February 20, 1988.

Her parents are Ronald Fenty and Monica Braithwaite. They separated when she was a teenager. Rihanna has two younger brothers, Rorrey and Rajad.

Rihanna, her brother Rajad (*left*), and her mother (*right*) attended Paris Fashion Week in 2015.

WHERE IN THE WORLD?

MARTINIQUE

CARIBBEAN
SEA

SAINT LUCIA

BARBADOS

SAINT VINCENT
AND THE
GRENADINES

Saint Michael Parish

GRANADA

N
W E
S

GROWING TALENT

From a young age, Rihanna loved to sing and **perform**. She listened to Caribbean music, **hip-hop**, and **rhythm and blues**.

As a teenager, Rihanna was in a music group called Contrast. At 15, she met an American music **producer**.

Together, they made her first album, *Music of the Sun*. It featured the single, "Pon de Replay." This song became a hit around the world.

"Pon de Replay" translates to *play it again*. This song was on Rihanna's audition tape for Jay Z.

After her audition, Jay Z immediately signed Rihanna to a recording contract.

RISING STAR

After her first album, Rihanna quickly became a **celebrity**. Her second album was called *A Girl Like Me*. Fans loved her song, "S.O.S." This was Rihanna's first song to top the Billboard chart.

In 2007, Rihanna **released** *Good Girl Gone Bad*. The album sold more than 5 million copies in the United States. The album's hit song, "Umbrella," featured **rapper** Jay Z.

DID YOU KNOW?

In 2008, Rihanna released hit singles "Take a Bow" and "Disturbia."

In 2008, Rihanna won a Grammy Award for "Umbrella."

Rihanna went through a hard time in 2009. Writing songs for *Rated R* helped her to feel better. Fans loved Rihanna's new sound.

Her music continued to change. Rihanna's *Loud* album included fun dance songs. **Rappers** Drake and Nicki Minaj were each featured in a song.

All of Rihanna's hard work paid off. In 2011, this album featured her tenth number-one Billboard chart song.

DID YOU KNOW?
In 2011, Rihanna became the youngest solo artist to have recorded ten number-one singles.

Rihanna traveled to Brazil to promote her album, *Loud*.

CONTINUED SUCCESS

In 2012, Rihanna **released** her seventh album. *Unapologetic* featured a song called "Stay." It was another hit.

Rihanna spent 2014 working on other projects. She did more acting. And, she sang with other artists on their records. She also joined **rapper** Eminem on a three-city tour.

In 2012, Rihanna sang in Berlin, Germany, on the 777 Tour. She performed 7 shows in 7 countries in 7 days!

Rihanna made more public appearances. In 2015, she sang "The Star-Spangled Banner" at a New York Mets baseball game.

After more than three years, fans were excited for a new Rihanna album. *Anti* was **released** in 2016. Within three months, it sold 2 million copies in the United States.

Rihanna collaborated with Kanye West (*right*) and Paul McCartney (*left*) on "FourFiveSeconds." They performed it for the first time at the 2015 Grammy Awards.

FASHION ICON

Rihanna is a fashion icon. She is known for wearing stylish clothes. And, she attends major fashion shows around the world.

As a trendsetter, Rihanna also designs for clothes brands. Fans love to buy goods Rihanna helped create!

Rihanna's Fenty Puma collection included sneakers.

In 2015, Rihanna attended the Met Gala in New York City, New York.

19

SOCIAL MEDIA

Rihanna is active on **social media**. This way, she can reach out to millions of fans. As of 2017, Rihanna has about 69 million Twitter followers. And, she has nearly 76 million fans on Facebook. People also watch Rihanna's music videos on YouTube.

In 2016, Rihanna took a selfie with fans at a Los Angeles Lakers basketball game.

AWARDS

Rihanna has won many **awards**. As of 2016, Rihanna has won eight **Grammy Awards**. In 2017, she was **nominated** for another eight awards!

Over the years, Rihanna has won many other awards. Some have been for music. One award was from the Council of Fashion Designers of America.

Rapper Drake presented Rihanna with the Michael Jackson Video Vanguard Award at the 2016 MTV Video Music Awards.

GIVING BACK

Rihanna gives her time and money to good causes. Her **charity** is called the Clara Lionel **Foundation**. It helps students from other countries go to school in the United States.

Around the world, people benefit from Rihanna's giving spirit. She has supplied food to those who lost everything during big storms. And, she gave money to a Barbados hospital.

Prince Harry met Rihanna during his tour of the Caribbean. They spread the word about an illness called AIDS.

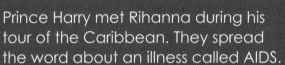

Rihanna worked with the Help a London Child charity in London, England.

ON SCREEN

Rihanna is often on TV. She has been a guest on *The Ellen Degeneres Show* and *Jimmy Kimmel Live!*

She starred in *Battleship*, an action movie. In 2014, Rihanna appeared in the musical *Annie*. The next year, she was a voice actor in *Home*.

Rihanna attended the *Home* premiere in Los Angeles, California.

BUZZ

Rihanna is one of the biggest **celebrities** in the world. In 2017, she is working on her ninth album. Rihanna is also continuing with her fashion line. Fans are excited to see what Rihanna does next!

Rihanna received the 2017 Harvard University Humanitarian of the Year Award.

GLOSSARY

award something that is given in recognition of good work or a good act.

celebrity a famous or celebrated person.

charity a group or a fund that helps people in need.

foundation (faun-DAY-shuhn) the base that helps support a building.

Grammy Award any of the awards given each year by the National Academy of Recording Arts and Sciences. Grammy Awards honor the year's best accomplishments in music.

hip-hop a form of popular music that features rhyme, spoken words, and electronic sounds. It is similar to rap music.

nominate to name as a possible winner.

perform to do something in front of an audience.

pop relating to popular music.

producer a person who oversees the making of a movie, a play, an album, or a radio or television show.

rapper someone who raps. To rap is to speak the words of a song to a beat.

release to make available to the public.

rhythm and blues (RIH-thuhm) a form of popular music that features a strong beat. It is inspired by jazz, gospel, and blues styles.

social media a form of communication on the internet where people can share information, messages, and videos. It may include blogs and online groups.

WEBSITES

To learn more about Pop Biographies, visit **abdobooklinks.com**.
These links are routinely monitored and updated to provide
the most current information available.

INDEX